MAUREEN ZAREMBA AND

KEVIN GREENE

D1710309

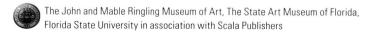

Grounds and Gardens
THE JOHN AND MABLE RINGLING MUSEUM OF ART ART SPACES

The John and Mable Ringling Museum of Art, The State Art Museum of Florida,
Florida State University in association with Scala Publishers

Introduction

Blessed with exceptional natural beauty, the city of Sarasota, on the Gulf Coast of Florida, has often been called a tropical paradise. Spectacular sunsets, award-winning white sand beaches, lush greenery, and a balmy climate have attracted visitors there for more than a century, including circus king, financier, and art collector, John Ringling (1866–1936), and his wife, Mable (1875–1929). The Ringlings' love of Sarasota was perhaps most clearly expressed by their decision to build the city a spectacular museum in which to house an outstanding collection of European art.

← Art museum and grounds

← John and Mable Ringling

→ Advertisement for
   Sarasota, 1924

⇢ Banyan tree

Set amidst beautiful grounds and gardens, The John and Mable Ringling Museum of Art is now home to multiple venues: an art museum with renowned Old Master paintings and growing contemporary collections; a circus museum dedicated to the history of the American circus; an elegant performance space known as the Historic Asolo Theater; and Ca' d'Zan, the Ringlings' spectacular, Gilded Age mansion. All of these buildings are enhanced by their location along the shores of Sarasota Bay.

As an enthusiastic gardener, Mable would be pleased to know that the grounds and gardens of the Ringling estate have grown into a park where visitors can spend the day smelling the roses and relaxing in the shade of the banyans. The Ringlings' original investment in their natural environment has been enhanced over the years by dedicated staff and volunteers, who invite you to explore this extraordinary collection of living treasures.

History

↑ Palms Elysian, *c.* 1910s

→ Palms Elysian, *c.* 1920s

In 1911, John and Mable Ringling purchased a house called Palms Elysian, as well as twenty acres of land on Sarasota Bay. This property was previously owned by Charles N. Thompson, a one-time manager of the Buffalo Bill Wild West Show. The Thompsons had tamed the area around the house, but indigenous plants such as cabbage palms, palmettos, and pines still covered much of the grounds. Soon after arriving in Sarasota, however, the Ringlings began to re-landscape the property, drawing attention from the local community. As early as 1913, newspaper reports were describing the "north shore beautification" taking place along Indian and Shell Beaches where the estate was located. Hedges were planted and palms were installed on the walkways and the waterside frontage, enhancing the view of Palms Elysian from the bay. The banyan trees that now dominate the grounds may also have been planted at this time.

While John traveled on business, Mable spent time in Sarasota, where she indulged her passion for plants, which life in a New York City apartment and luxurious private railcar had not previously allowed. In addition to basic landscaping, she oversaw the construction

JOHN RINGLING'S WINTER HOME, NEAR SARASOTA, FLA.

↑ Rose Garden, *c.* 1910s

↗ Mable on the grounds

two new gardens on the estate. The first was the Rose Garden, completed in 1913. Likely inspired by gardens the Ringlings had seen on trips to Europe, it consisted of a wide variety of roses laid out in a formal design. The second was the Secret Garden, comprising a less formal arrangement of plants given as gifts to Mable by her friends and neighbors. Both gardens probably served as restful retreats where Mable could catch her breath between her many personal and civic engagements.

The Ringlings eventually replaced Palms Elysia with a Venetian Gothic-style mansion, named Ca' d'Zan or "House of John," built between 1924–26. The hous served as a winter residence, where the Ringlings coul entertain wealthy individuals interested in supportin John's efforts to transform Sarasota from a sma seaside town to an international vacation destinatio

← Secret Garden, *c.* 1920s

S. 56—Entrance to John Ringling Mansion, Sarasota, Fla.

← Ca' d'Zan, c. 1920s

← Ca' d'Zan gatehouse, c. 1930s

Driveway,
John Ringling's Home,
Sarasota, Fla.

↑ Drive to Ca' d'Zan, *c.* 1930s

→ Front lawn of Ca' d'Zan

↠ Art museum courtyard,
  c. 1930s

Visitors approached Ca' d'Zan through an elegant gate-house, of similar style, and down a drive surrounded by lush, sub-tropical plants. An impressive, palm-lined walk with a terra-cotta mosaic depicting signs of the zodiac framed the house, while a white marble swimming pool and a variety of exotic trees punctuated the expansive front lawn.

Following the completion of Ca' d'Zan, construction began on the art museum in 1927. Inspired by Renaissance

↑ Art museum courtyard,
 c. 1920s

→ Original Dwarf Garden and
 Historic Asolo Theater, *c.*
 1950s

villas the Ringlings had seen while traveling in Italy, th
museum was designed as a U-shaped structure with
central courtyard, which offered Mable an opportunit
to create a formal setting that embodied the ideals o
Renaissance garden design. Sadly, this was to prove he
final landscaping project, for she died in 1929.

The estate became the property of the State o
Florida in 1946. Then lush with palms, pines, banyan
bougainvillea, and hibiscus, the grounds were in need o
attention after the benign neglect that followed John
death ten years earlier. Under the first director of Th
John and Mable Ringling Museum of Art, A. Evere
"Chick" Austin, Jr. (1946–57), the plants were tame
and the lawns were manicured. Austin's successor, Ke
neth Donahue (1957–64), initiated landscaping projec
that framed the buildings and enhanced the statua
placed around the estate. Donahue was also able
realize Austin's vision of a separate building for the Hi
toric Asolo Theater, which came to the Museum in 195
The Dwarf Garden consisting of a group of stone statue
of dwarfs surrounding a central fountain connected th
theater to the art museum.

← Millennium Tree Trail

⬅ Bolger Promenade and
   Bolger Campiello

In 2000, the Museum partnered with the National Arbor Day Foundation to create the Millennium Tree Trail. Marking the southern boundary of the Museum's property, this scenic walk is dedicated to displaying native trees that provide visitors with a shady respite from the summer sun. A master plan was developed in 2009 to inform the future growth of the Museum and to ensure the continued beauty of the estate. Part of this vision was the palm-lined promenade and paved *campiello* (small square) situated along the water's edge, funded by philanthropist David F. Bolger. From this magnificent vantage point, visitors can look out across the bay to the keys that once belonged to John Ringling. The current planting program is designed to enhance the collection of exotic trees on the estate while also maintaining the native species of Florida's sub-tropical environment, ensuring that the Museum's grounds and gardens remain an important part of the visitor experience for generations to come.

↑ A rose in bloom

→ Layout of the Rose Garden

Rose Garden

Mable Ringling's first major landscaping project involved the design and installation of a formal rose garden. Completed in 1913, this 27,000-square-foot garden was located within a short walk of the Ringlings' home. Occupying what was likely the site of an earlier garden, it was laid out in a formal, wagon-wheel design that Mable had probably seen on trips to Italy. Beds of roses are arranged in concentric circles around a central point at which is poised a Classical *tempietto*, or temple-like structure, topped by a wrought iron canopy. Like the spokes of a wheel, shell paths radiate out from this gazebo at regular intervals. The entire garden is bounded by a pergola of concrete pillars that at one time supported a flowering vine, most likely jasmine, which would have provided shade and added scent to the already fragrant setting. Stone sculptures of courting couples, purchased by the Ringlings in Europe, add a further decorative note.

Rose gardening in Florida in the early 1900s proved challenging, as roses are prone to a variety of pests, including nematodes, wormlike creatures that attack

← Rose Garden

rosebush roots. While roses grown in Florida today are grafted onto pest-resistant root stock, Mable's early solution to maintaining healthy plants was a regimen of "root pruning," in which bushes were regularly dug up and replaced.

Though none of Mable's original rose bushes survive, many of the 1,200 roses currently growing in the garden are of the same types as those planted by her. They include numerous varieties, such as hybrid teas, floribundas, grandifloras, and old garden roses, dating back to as early as 1751. One rose, developed by a member of the Museum's staff, is dedicated to Mable. Accredited by All-American Rose Selections, the garden was named the most outstanding All-American Rose Selections Public Rose Garden in 2006.

Secret Garden

Directly to the north of Ca' d'Zan is an area now referred to as Mable Ringling's Secret Garden. Historic photographs of the property suggest the presence of a previously existing garden, so it is likely that Mable built her new garden over the old one. Here Mable placed specimen plants, referred to as "onesies and twosies," presented to her by friends and guests. She is likely to have returned such favors with cuttings of her own, as is customary among gardeners. Crushed shell paths allow for walking and working among the beds, while a surrounding hedge provides a degree of privacy. Contemporary references describe the garden as an outdoor retreat where Mable could take a break from the demands of her role as a society hostess.

After Mable's death, the garden suffered from neglect and rapidly became overgrown. Thankfully, it was revived with help from the Driftwood Circle of the Sarasota Garden Club. It is apt that this organization, of which Mable was the first president, played such a significant role in restoring her former refuge. The current look and feel of the Secret Garden is very much in keeping with Mable's informal, eclectic approach.

→ Secret Garden

↑ Mable in her garden

→ Secret Garden

Arranged around a large decorative urn are beds filled with a diverse and colorful mix of bromeliads, shrubs, roses, succulents, periwinkles, and other Florida friendly varieties.

Just beyond the garden is a private enclosure in which the Ringlings are buried together with John's sister, Ida. While the Ringlings had originally planned to be buried in an elaborate crypt underneath the bridge at the west end of the courtyard of the art museum, the project was incomplete at the time of Mable's death and never finished. Given her love of nature, it is perhaps more fitting that she should be laid to rest near the garden she created.

Art Museum Courtyard

In the late nineteenth and early twentieth centuries, many of America's greatest collectors considered the Italian Renaissance the high point of Western civilization. Isabella Stewart Gardner, John Pierpont Morgan and Henry Walters, among others, identified themselves with their Renaissance predecessors, displaying their

→ Ringling burial site

⇢ Art museum courtyard

↑ Art museum courtyard

→ Reproduction of the Turtle Fountain

fabulous works of art in museums designed to look lik Renaissance palaces. John Ringling's Renaissance-styl museum took the form of a U-shaped structure with lon loggias flanking a central courtyard. The latter serve as an extension of the surrounding galleries, as well a an exhibition space in itself. It is the setting for an arra of bronze and stone copies of famous Classical, Renais sance, and Baroque sculptures, the majority of whic John purchased from the Chiurazzi Foundry in Naples.

The art museum courtyard embodies many of th ideals of a true Renaissance garden. According to th writer and architect, Leon Battista Alberti (1404–72 the perfect garden should be enclosed within a cour yard bound by porticos, yet open to the sun and coolin breezes with paths and plantings laid out in straig lines and circles, forming basic geometric designs. should also include water features, the sound of whic could sooth visitors.

Transformed from Florida swampland, the courtya consists of three tiered terraces linked by a centr staircase. Each terrace is divided into regular section reflecting the symmetry and proportion indicative of th

← Pine trees in the courtyard

⇐ Reproduction of the
  Oceanus Fountain

Renaissance. The upper terrace is divided into twelve beds, or parterres, covered with turf and low-growing juniper. Each parterre features a cast of a Classical statue that rises up out of the greenery. To these have been added reproductions of Giacomo della Porta's Fontane delle Tartarughe (Turtle Fountain) from the Piazza Mattei in Rome and Giambologna's Oceanus Fountain from the Boboli Gardens in Florence. The middle terrace is punctuated by native slash pines. Legend has it that Mable Ringling insisted these trees be saved when the courtyard was being constructed. She was likely aware of the popularity of such trees in the gardens she visited in Italy. The lower terrace is divided into grass lawn featuring additional casts of Classical statues. At the west end is a splendid water feature, consisting of a moat flanked by statues of reclining figures representing the Nile and Tiber, the great rivers of Egypt and Rome. The overall arrangement is similar to that found at the Villa Lante in Italy, home to what many experts consider to be the quintessential Renaissance garden.

The loggias lining the courtyard to the north, south and east are bounded by an ornamental balustrade

← Water feature in the courtyard

⟵ Cast of the figure of the Nile (top); cast of the figure of the Tiber (bottom)

→ Oil jar with bougainvillea

interrupted at regular intervals by Italian olive oil jars planted with brightly colored bougainvillea. Surmounting a bridge at the west end of the courtyard is a cast of Michelangelo's David, one of the most famous of all Renaissance sculptures. Towering above David are elegant royal palms, indicative of Florida's sub-tropical landscape.

The courtyard was an essential part of the Ringlings' vision for the art museum. Though the sculptures have been moved and many of the original plants have been replaced, the experience of the courtyard remains essentially the same today as in the Ringlings' day.

← Cast of David with
   royal palms

Dwarf Garden

In 1958, the Museum's second director, Kenneth Donahue, created the Dwarf Garden in between the art museum and the building then housing the Historic Asolo Theater, an eighteenth-century Italian theater acquired in 1950 by the first director, Chick Austin. The word "Dwarf," in this case, does not refer to the plants in the garden, but to the whimsical limestone statues of *commedia dell'arte* players found there. The *commedia* was a type of improvisational theater developed in Italy in the sixteenth and seventeenth centuries. The figures in the garden were likely a nod to the theater next door,

← Dwarf Garden

→ Millennium Tree Trail

which was brought to Sarasota from its original home i
Asolo, Italy. They would certainly have amused theate
patrons waiting to see a show.

When the Historic Asolo Theater was reinstalled i
the new Visitor Pavilion in 2006, the Dwarf Garden wa
moved to its present location adjacent to the Children
Welcome Center. The dwarfs themselves line a circula
path that passes beneath a banyan tree. Peeking o
from among various sub-tropical plants, such as bro
meliads, hibiscus, bamboo, and orchids, these comic
characters continue to delight visitors of all ages.

Millennium Tree Trail

To mark the year 2000, the Museum created the Mille
nium Tree Trail, a shady walk on the southern edge o
the property that provides a welcome respite from th
intense Florida sun. The trail showcases a wide variet
of local and regional trees, including oak, holly, citru
and magnolia, which thrive in Florida's sub-tropic
climate. These trees are displayed in native habitat

ranging from swampy to coastal. The result is a tapestry of rough and smooth barks, large and small leaves, and a palette of different greens. As an educational installation, the trail serves as both a resource for local gardeners looking for ideas to implement at home, and an introduction to indigenous species for visitors from outside Florida. To help differentiate a palm from a palmetto, the specimens are labeled with both their botanical and common names.

← Millennium Tree Trail

It is a symbol of happiness, prosperity, longevity, and good luck. Bo trees are related to banyans, but do not grow as large. They produce figs, and their leaves turn from purple to green as they mature. *Native to: India and Asia*

Bombax Tree *(Bombax ceiba), also known as Red Cotton Tree and Silk-Cotton Tree*

The bombax tree is a real showstopper when in full bloom, usually around late February to early March. Once finished flowering, the tree may produce fruit capsules filled with a silky substance that drifts when released into the air. The trunk of the tree is covered with conical thorns that give it a primeval appearance. While most bombax trees grow straight upwards, the estate's tilts sideways, having fallen over when it was young. *Native to: Southern China / Indo-Malaysia*

Cabbage Palm *(Sabal palmetto)*

The cabbage palm is the official state tree of Florida. More than 650 of these trees can be found on the estate. Some are known to pre-date the Ringlings. *Native to: North America*

← Cabbage palm

⇐ Bombax tree

Royal Poinciana *(Delonix regia)*
Royal poincianas are at their best in the spring when they are covered in orange flowers. The trees are legumes, which mean they produce bean pods that grow to about eight inches in length. *Native to: Madagascar*

↑ Fruit of the sausage tree

→ Sausage tree

Sausage Tree *(Kigelia pinnata)*
Sausage trees take their name from their fruits, which resemble sausages hanging on long cords. The trees have unique, claret-colored flowers with deep throats, which open at night and are pollinated by bats.
Native to: Tropical Africa

Shaving Brush Tree *(Pseudobombax ellipticum)*
Shaving brush trees derive their name from their flowers, which look like shaving brushes when fully open. When in bloom, the trees are completely covered in these flowers, which are a vibrant pink with yellow pollen tips. After flowering has finished, the trees set new leaves that turn from purple to green as they mature.
Native to: Mexico and Guatemala

← Shaving brush tree

Text and Photography
Copyright © 2013
The John and Mable Ringling
Museum of Art
Copyright © Scala Arts
Publishers, Inc. 2013

First published in 2013 by
Scala Arts Publishers, Inc
141 Wooster Street
New York, NY 10012, USA
www.scalapublishers.com
Scala • New York • London

in association with
The John and Mable Ringling
Museum of Art

ISBN: 978-1-85759-782-0

Edited by Stephanie Emerson
Designed by Inglis Design
Produced by © Scala Arts
Publishers, Inc.

Printed and bound in China
10 9 8 7 6 5 4 3 2 1

Front cover:
Statue in the Rose Garden

Back cover:
Oil jar with bougainvillea

All images are courtesy
The John and Mable Ringling
Museum of Art.